House System Magic:
Easy 10-Step Guide to School Spirit

Tailis Oniwon

DEDICATION

This book is for my children. Everything that I do is for you.

This book is also dedicated to the educators who make school a safe place for students, despite a climate that doesn't always value educators.

Finally, it is dedicated to my husband, Asuku, for always supporting my dreams.

CONTENTS

ACKNOWLEDGMENTS

I am profoundly grateful to everyone who has supported me throughout the journey of writing this book.

First and foremost, I want to thank my family. To my wonderful husband, Asuku, thank you for your support and encouragement. To my four beautiful children, everything I do is for you. Your love and patience have been my greatest source of strength.

A heartfelt thank you to my Crockett team. I could not accomplish anything on campus without you. We are fortunate to have such excellent educators.

I want to thank my PTO and parent volunteers for dedicating hours of their personal time to make our house system a success.

I would also like to acknowledge my colleagues and mentors for their guidance and inspiration. Your wisdom and experience have shaped this book in countless ways.

To Mrs. Adame, thank you for everything you have done for both our campus and for me. Your hard work has freed some of my time to dedicate to these projects.

To Dr. Washington, thank you for keeping me on my toes grammatically and for being a valuable sounding board.

Lastly, I want to express my gratitude to all the educators who inspire me daily. Your dedication and passion for teaching are the heart of this book.

Thank you all for being a part of this journey. This book would not have been possible without your support and encouragement.

.

1 DISCOVER YOUR WHY UNCOVERING THE PURPOSE BEHIND YOUR HOUSE SYSTEM

Hi there! My name is Tailis Oniwon, and for the past four years, I've had the incredible honor of being the principal at Crockett Elementary in Baytown, TX. Before taking on the principal role, I spent three years as an administrator in my district, and I've been in the wild, wonderful world of education for 14 years.

Now, let me tell you a little about my other full-time job: parenting. I have four amazing kids, aged 17, 16, 7, and 2. Yes, you read that right. Life at home is a constant adventure, filled with teenage drama, middle school milestones, and toddler tantrums. It keeps me on my toes and reminds me daily of the joys and challenges our students bring to school.

Why do I do what I do? Because I absolutely love it. There's nothing quite like the thrill of seeing a child's eyes light up when they finally "get it" or the satisfaction of knowing I've played a part in shaping their future. Sure, some days are tougher than others (okay, many days), but I consider myself incredibly blessed to be in a position to make a difference.

I wrote this guide with the hope that it helps you navigate the wonderful chaos of implementing a house system in your school. It's packed with practical tips and plenty of room for your own notes. My goal is to help you create a positive, engaging environment for your students and staff.

So, dive in, take notes, and let's make an impact together!

Discover Your Why

If you're doing the math, you'll realize I started as a principal right in the thick of COVID. Yes, a brand-new principal at the height of mask mandates and utter chaos. And if that wasn't enough, I walked into a turnover situation with 22 new staff members, including myself and a brand-new assistant principal. Talk about jumping into the deep end!

As an administrator, I've always valued a positive culture. But here I was, new to the campus, brand new to the principalship, smack in the middle of a pandemic where we couldn't gather, be close, or team build. Students had been isolated at home for months, and the challenge was clear: How could I build community in our school during these difficult times?

While researching different ideas, I came across the Ron Clark House System. I'll be honest—it seemed like a lot. Many public schools simply don't have the resources to pull this off. This is not a dig at the academy; I truly admire the work they're doing and have enjoyed Ron Clark's books. I aspire to that level of excellence. However, with a full house of children and starting in the pandemic, I needed to scale this way back.

Even with the upcoming practical tips, it may seem like a lot for some. I challenge you to truly do what works for you, your campus, and your budget. House systems can be fun without trying to keep up with what you see from other campuses. Do what works for you.

Here is where I challenge you to think about your why. Why do you want to embark on this journey? I truly believe in being intentional and not adding onto the plates of our already overworked educators unnecessarily. My why was wanting to find a fun and engaging way to bring the school community together during a very difficult time. It needs to make sense to you, and you need to be able to sell the need to the people who will implement it. Without that, there will be no buy-in.

House System Magic: Easy 10-Step Guide to School Spirit

Discover Your Why Uncovering the Purpose Behind Your House System

Questions for Reflection:
1. What is your primary motivation for implementing a house system in your school?

2. How do you envision the house system improving your school's culture?

3. What specific challenges are you facing that a house system could help address?

4. How can you adapt the house system to fit your school's unique needs and resources?

5. Who will be your key supporters in implementing this system, and how will you gain their buy-in?

6. How will you measure the success of the house system once it's implemented?

7. What steps can you take to ensure the house system is sustainable in the long term?

Reflect on these questions and write down your thoughts. Your "why" will be the foundation that supports your house system and helps you stay focused on your goals.

2 HOUSE NUMBERS AND NAMES CRAFTING IDENTITY: NAMING AND NUMBERING YOUR HOUSES

The first step in this house system journey was to choose our house names. Now, don't get me wrong—we love the Ron Clark house names. We even have a soft spot for the Harry Potter names. Shout out to House Gryffindor! But we wanted names that would resonate with even our youngest kiddos (think five-year-olds). We aimed for cool, exciting names that students would be thrilled to be a part of.

Our PBIS team rolled up their sleeves and got to work drafting our names and images. This is a great place where you could get students involved. Unfortunately, during COVID, we didn't have students on campus for months and couldn't involve them in this fun process. But under normal circumstances, involving students can make a huge difference in getting them pumped about the new system.

We have around 600 students, so we decided to go with four houses. This will totally depend on your school's size and needs. I've seen campuses with six, eight, and even more houses. The key is to find what works best for your community.

Drumroll, please... Our house names are Wakanda (Panther), Ignite (Phoenix), Lightning (Pegasus), and Aragon (Dragon). Pretty cool, right? The goal is to make your houses fun and relevant, so students are excited to be a part of them. Remember, if the students aren't feeling it, the system won't fly.

Biggest Tip: Make your houses fun, relevant, and something students will want to be part of. This is the foundation for creating enthusiasm and engagement.

This image was created by ChatGPT. It illustrates how easy it can be to get a design if you don't have designers in your building.

House Numbers and Names Crafting Identity: Naming and Numbering Your Houses

Questions for Reflection:
1. What themes or elements are most likely to resonate with your student population?

2. How many houses will work best for your school's size and structure?

3. What images or symbols will make your house names come alive for students?

4. How can you involve students in the naming process to ensure buy-in and excitement?

5. How can you ensure that house names and symbols reflect diversity and inclusivity?

6. What steps will you take to introduce the house names to the students and staff?

7. How will you incorporate house names and imagery into the school culture and environment?

3 CHARACTER TRAITS AND PBIS BUILDING CHARACTER: INTEGRATING POSITIVE BEHAVIORAL INTERVENTIONS AND SUPPORTS

Your houses should stand for something. They can't just be fun names. Remember what I said about being intentional and knowing your why? The house system should be an integral part of your everyday PBIS (Positive Behavioral Interventions and Supports) system. The key is to incorporate it into what you're already doing, not to make it one more thing on your plate.

Each of our houses symbolizes a character trait that is important to our campus. Wakanda is the house of courage. Ignite is the house of perseverance. Aragon is the house of respect. Lightning is the house of kindness. These traits aren't chosen at random—they align with the goals in our campus improvement plan.

Every month, our district celebrates one of these character traits and more. We tie our houses into this celebration, reinforcing the traits we want to cultivate in our students. For example, when the trait of the month is courage, we highlight the achievements of the students in the House of Wakanda. It's a great way to keep the focus on positive behavior while building house spirit.

By aligning your house traits with your school's goals and PBIS system, you create a cohesive and intentional framework that supports student development and school culture. This integration helps ensure that the house system is not just an add-on but a seamless part of your school's daily life.

Character Traits and PBIS Building Character: Integrating Positive Behavioral Interventions and Supports

Questions for Reflection:
1. What character traits are most important for your school to emphasize?

2. How do these traits align with your school's goals and improvement plan?

3. How can you incorporate your house system into your existing PBIS framework?

4. How will you celebrate and highlight each character trait throughout the year?

5. How can you involve students and staff in promoting and modeling these traits?

6. What resources or activities can you use to reinforce the character traits in each house?

7. How will you measure the impact of emphasizing these traits on your school culture?

Reflect on these questions and consider how you can make your house system a meaningful part of your PBIS strategy. By doing so, you'll create a positive and supportive environment that encourages students to embody the values your school stands for.

4 HOUSE LEADERS EMPOWERING LEADERSHIP: SELECTING AND TRAINING HOUSE LEADERS

The people who lead your houses will determine how much energy and enthusiasm your house system has. Ideally, these leaders would be on your PBIS committee. Within our PBIS committee, we have a house planning subcommittee. This ensures that we have dedicated time and resources to make our house system successful.

House Planning Subcommittee

Campus Leadership Team: Our house planning subcommittee consists of four members of our campus leadership team:

- The assistant principal
- Our campus student success specialist (formerly called family involvement coordinator)
- The counselor
- Myself (the principal)

Each of us leads one house to ensure each house has an administrator. This helps maintain consistency and support across the houses.

Teacher Leaders

Your teacher leaders can be volunteers or assigned as house leaders. The key is to choose people who are enthusiastic and willing to participate actively in rallies and help make spirit week a success. These leaders should be able to motivate students and foster a sense of community within their houses.

Selecting Teacher Leaders:

- Volunteers: Look for teachers who are excited about the house system and willing to take on the extra responsibility.
- Assigned Leaders: If you don't have enough volunteers, consider assigning leaders based on their strengths and interests.

Student Leaders

In addition to staff, we use students who are already members of our campus leadership teams. Remember what I said about using systems that are already in place? We already have a student council, AVID ambassadors, and a tech team. We utilize students who are already in leadership positions to assist with rally planning and implementation.

Involving Student Leaders:

- Student Council: Members can help with planning and promoting events.

- AVID Ambassadors: These students can assist with logistics and organizing activities.
- Tech Team: They can manage the technical aspects of rallies, such as sound and presentations.

Making It Work

Hype and Participation: The success of your house system depends on the energy and enthusiasm of your leaders. They should be actively involved in promoting house activities, encouraging participation, and fostering a positive atmosphere.

Spirit Week: House leaders play a crucial role in making spirit week a success. They should help organize activities, decorate the campus, and encourage students to participate. The more excitement they generate, the more engaged your students will be.

House Leaders Empowering Leadership: Selecting and Training House Leaders

Questions for Reflection:
1. Who are the most enthusiastic and motivated staff members to lead your houses?

2. How can you involve existing student leaders in your house system?

3. What strategies can you use to ensure house leaders are actively promoting and participating in house activities?

4. How will you support house leaders in their roles to ensure they have the resources and time they need?

5. What incentives or recognition can you provide to house leaders to keep them motivated?

6. How can you measure the impact of house leaders on the success of your house system?

7. How will you handle the transition of leadership if a house leader leaves or steps down?

Reflect on these questions to ensure you have the right leaders in place to make your house system a dynamic and engaging part of your school culture.

5 ASSIGNING HOUSES THE ASSIGNMENT PUZZLE: STRATEGICALLY PLACING STUDENTS IN HOUSES

Alright, now let's dive into the fun (and sometimes chaotic) process of assigning houses. This chapter will break down our methods, including tips and tricks to make your house selection day a memorable event.

Getting Started: The Initial Assignment

When we first started, remember we were in COVID times. We had teachers stand six feet apart and used an online randomized wheel. You could totally do this. It's not extremely exciting, but it is easy and gets the job done. Remember, do what works best for you.

House Selection Rally

Within the first three weeks of school, we rent a giant slide and hold our house selection rally. Students go down the slide, and at the end, they reach into a house cup and select their house card. They do not get to trade, which can lead to some tears. But hey, that's part of the excitement!

Step-by-Step Process:

1. Preparation: Before the big day, we download rosters into Excel and create a dropdown section with the house names.
2. Selection: As students go down the slide and pick their house card, they tell their name to one of the three staff members with iPads and show the card. They simply touch the dropdown next to the child's name and select the house. Super fast and easy!
3. Organization: Students go down by homeroom to make this process smoother. The first time will take the longest, but once students are in a house, they stay in that house forever.
4. Subsequent Years: In future years, only new staff and students go down the slide. Returning students sit in their house sections and cheer on the new members.

The Big Day

The house selection day should be exciting. We have our campus cheerleaders hyping it up, and we invite the high school dancers and cheerleaders to come out. This is all held during PE time on a Friday. All students go to PE that day, and music, art, PE teacher aides, and available staff help facilitate.

House Spirit Week: The week of house selection is dedicated as house spirit week. Each day leading up to the selection day is assigned to a house. Teachers and students in that house dress up and decorate the campus in their colors, creating excitement.

Daily Schedule:

- Monday: Ignite
- Tuesday: Lightning
- Wednesday: Aragon
- Thursday: Wakanda
- Friday: House Selection Day

On the announcements, we discuss the house, its colors, motto, animal, and trait for that day. Teams play pranks on each other, dress in their colors, and more.

Other Considerations

Before placing the house slips in the cup (essentially a huge trophy), check your spreadsheet to see how many students are already in each house per grade level and print accordingly. You don't want a house to be extremely stacked on house rally days in a grade level. If you are initially starting out, be sure to evenly print houses based on your student population.

House Colors/Shirts: Since students wear their house colors or shirts on selection day, we ask that parents have new students who aren't in a house wear a white shirt that can be written on that day. This is optional but helpful.

New Students

When we have a student enroll after house selection day, the counselor has them draw a house from the cup. It's a simple and fair way to integrate new members throughout the year.

House System Magic: Easy 10-Step Guide to School Spirit

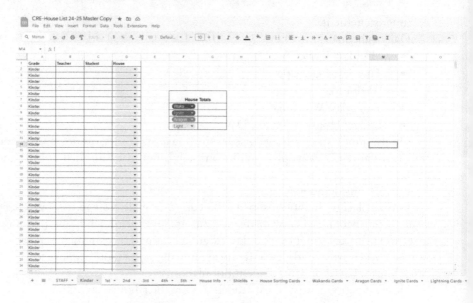

House System Magic: Easy 10-Step Guide to School Spirit

Assigning Houses The Assignment Puzzle: Strategically Placing Students in Houses

Questions for Reflection:
1. What method will you use to initially assign houses to teachers and students?

2. How will you make the house selection day exciting and memorable for your students?

3. What logistical steps will you take to ensure the house selection process runs smoothly?

4. How can you involve the entire school community in house spirit week?

5. How will you ensure that the distribution of students across houses is balanced?

6. What steps will you take to welcome new students into the house system after the initial selection day?

7. How will you maintain enthusiasm and participation in the house system throughout the school year?

Reflect on these questions and plan out your house assignment process to make it as fun and effective as possible. Your goal is to create a sense of belonging and excitement from day one!

6 POINTS EARNING SUCCESS: IMPLEMENTING A REWARDING POINTS SYSTEM

Tracking house points should be simple, fun, and efficient. We use Class Dojo to keep track of points, and the best part? It's easy and free! Class Dojo can be downloaded as an app on phones, tablets, and computers. If you're not familiar with Class Dojo, it's a breeze to learn. You select a "student" (in this case, it's houses), and when you click on an icon, it gives you options for points.

Here's a breakdown of the point options we have listed:
- Being Respectful
- Being Kind
- Persevering
- Being Courageous
- Spirit Wear (we give students a point for having "extra spirit" on rally days, which we'll discuss in the rally chapter)
- Rally Points
- Cafeteria Behavior
- Dismissal Behavior

All of these are worth one point, with the exception of cafeteria and dismissal behavior, which are worth five points since these are our campus hot spots. Anytime a teacher sees a student exhibiting these traits, they can ask them what house they are in or look at their backpack tag (see later in the miscellaneous chapter) and award a point to that house for the behavior.

Using Class Dojo

Step-by-Step Process:
1. Setup: Ensure every staff member joins our Dojo class as a teacher so they can award points. This is part of our back-to-school to-do list.
2. Awarding Points: Teachers can group students by houses for class activities and reward points for exhibiting desired behaviors or winning a challenge. The possibilities are endless.
3. Real-Time Tracking: Students love that "ding" when a point is awarded. It's an instant recognition that boosts morale and engagement.

Managing Points

Each nine weeks, we "clear" the points, but we make sure to list the points on our Word table so we know who the winner is at the end of the year. This system helps maintain a fresh start each term while still recognizing overall achievement.

House System Magic: Easy 10-Step Guide to School Spirit

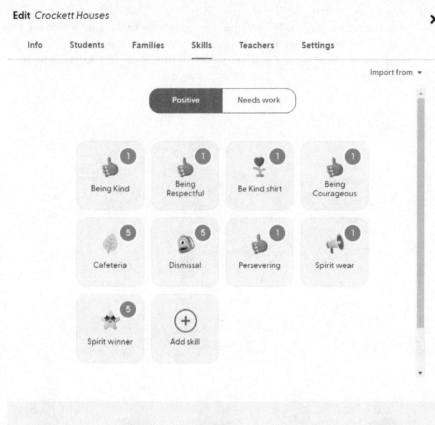

Edit *Crockett Houses*   ✕

Info   Students   Families   **Skills**   Teachers   Settings

Import from ▾

| Positive | Needs work |

- Being Kind
- Being Respectful
- Be Kind shirt
- Being Courageous
- Cafeteria
- Dismissal
- Persevering
- Spirit wear
- Spirit winner
- Add skill

Whole Class   House A   House I   House L   House W

23-24

	1st 9 weeks	2nd 9 weeks	3rd 9 weeks	4th 9 weeks	End of year total
Wakanda	1495	1919	1821	1332	6567
ignite	1553	1937	1626	850	5966
Aragon	1485	1902	1864	785	6036
lightning	1478	1996	1913	963	6350

House System Magic: Easy 10-Step Guide to School Spirit

Points Earning Success: Implementing a Rewarding Points System

Questions for Reflection:
1. What behaviors are most important for your school to recognize and reward?

2. How will you ensure all staff members are familiar with using Class Dojo?

3. What strategies can you use to incorporate house points into your existing PBIS framework?

4. How will you celebrate and recognize house achievements throughout the year?

5. What processes will you put in place to ensure points are awarded fairly and consistently?

6. How can you involve students in the process of tracking and celebrating house points?

7. How will you handle the clearing and recording of points each term to maintain motivation?

Reflect on these questions to fine-tune your point system and ensure it's both effective and engaging for your school community.

7 RALLIES UNIFYING MOMENTS: PLANNING EXCITING HOUSE RALLIES

House rallies can be a blast. They can also be very stressful. We are still actively tweaking our process and coming up with different ideas as we go. Here's a rundown of what works for us and some tips to help you plan your own exciting house rallies.

Rally Schedule
Frequency and Timing: We have five rallies throughout the year. The first is the selection rally within the first three weeks of school. The next three are standard rallies every nine weeks. The last rally is a house celebration where, instead of competing against the other houses, students spend time with their house members in rotations to bond. This is also when the overall winner is announced.

Ideal Timing: We love Fridays! Even better are half days for students. Our teachers' conference time is one hour, so we schedule rally times based on their allotted times for conferences. This means teachers decide if they will attend, as I believe in not interrupting instructional minutes unless necessary. Some campuses have all students attend a huge rally, but we don't have the space to accommodate this. Instead, we hold three different rallies, which works great for half days. If not on half days, we hold them on Fridays. Instead of running six different specials rotations that day (K-5), we hold three, grouped as K-1, 2-3, and 4-5. This also allows us to adjust our games by attention span and ability.

Planning and Preparation
Using a Shared Google Doc: To plan the games, we use a shared Google Doc where the house subcommittee can input game ideas, materials needed, and other suggestions. This method minimizes unnecessary meetings and keeps everything organized. I believe in the "it could've been an email" philosophy, so our campus committees meet once a month instead of having faculty meetings. Each committee addresses a specific area of the school, with every team represented. PBIS members share input for rallies, and coaches, as part of the house planning committee, often have fun and effective game ideas. I listed our actual planning document below so you can see the good, bad, and ugly of the planning process and thought processes.

House System Magic: Easy 10-Step Guide to School Spirit

Rally Execution

Welcoming Students: When students enter, they sit with their house. Cheerleaders welcome them at the entrance and hype them up. Music plays on the loudspeaker, and every section is decorated with house banners and other items. We usually have balloon arches and even a life-size standing cardboard Black Panther for Wakanda. It gets competitive! We also purchase pompoms clappers, and other pep-rally style items in bulk in each house color to use for rallies.

Hosting and Facilitating: Although I attend every rally, hosting them all can be difficult. We assign a different administrator to host each rally and a teacher leader to help facilitate. The music, art, PE teachers, and PE aide also help, along with all available paras.

Rally Activities:
1. Introduction (10 minutes): Once all students are seated, we review the purpose of the house system. Each house does their "move," and a student from each house shares an example of how they exhibited their house's character trait that nine weeks.
2. Teacher Game (3-5 minutes): Teachers compete in a game, earning rally points for their house.
3. Student Games (30-35 minutes): We select students to compete in various games. It's important to choose games that are easy to facilitate and allow multiple students to play. Not all students may get to play, so it's important to give points for sportsmanship and encourage everyone to cheer on their house.
4. Spirit Stick Competition (5 minutes): We hold the spirit stick over each house and see who can be the loudest with the most spirit. The winning house gets a spirit point and keeps the spirit stick for the next nine weeks.
5. Announcing the Winner: We announce the nine weeks' winner, and that house receives a treat on the way out. Treats are usually bought in bulk to be cost-effective. At the end of the year, the house with the most cumulative points gets their house name etched onto the house cup for the school year, and every student in that house gets a medal (bought in bulk from Amazon).

Managing Downtime

Cheerleaders and Student Leaders: To avoid dead time, cheerleaders perform cheers while student leaders and specials teachers set up and remove game materials. This keeps the energy high and the transitions smooth.

Parent Involvement: We send a message to parents asking them to have students show extra spirit (face paint, hair color, etc.). Teachers award points to students' houses for showing up with extra flare. We also have PTO members and Watch D.O.G.S. (Dads Of Great Students) volunteer to assist with rallies, helping with setup, supervision, and cleanup. Their involvement adds another layer of excitement and community spirit.

Rally Logistics

Pre-Rally Setup: Before rallies, our cheerleaders, student leaders, and specials teachers bring out all the equipment needed and line them up based on the order of the games. Between games, while cheerleaders are cheering, they remove materials from the previous games and set up for the next game. At the end, they assist with clean-up.

Sample Rally Schedule: Here's an example of how we structure our rallies:
- 10 minutes: Introduction and purpose of the system.
- 5 minutes: House "moves" and student examples of character traits.
- 3-5 minutes: Teacher game.
- 30-35 minutes: Student games.
- 5 minutes: Spirit stick competition and announcement of the winner.

Treats and Rewards: If divided equally, we usually have about 150 members per house. We typically buy treats in bulk from Sam's Club, such as fruit snacks or Rice Krispies treats. We have a line item for these treats in our PTO budget, and it is relatively inexpensive. Students get bragging rights and treats for their house's achievements.

House System Magic: Easy 10-Step Guide to School Spirit

Shared Planning Document:
This is our actual shared document with notes that our house committee uses for planning. The good, bad and ugly.

October 13th House Rally
Setup: 8:05 AM
- AVID Ambassadors, paras, and leadership (specials conference)
- Setup: 4 corners, hang banners, and spirit out (how can we make this better?)

Rally Schedule:
- K/1st: 8:45-9:30
- 2nd/3rd: 9:40-10:25
- 4th/5th: 10:35-11:20

Game/Order	Person Responsible	Items Needed	Time Needed	Notes
Welcome	Welcome Teacher Rep/Oniwon	Music - Bear	10 minutes	
Review of Expectations and Houses				Give house points to groups if following the expectations.
Current Point Standing		Promethean		
Teacher Game		Cup game for teachers	3 minutes	
Game 1: Rock Paper Scissors Hula Hoop Jump		Hula Hoops	5 minutes	
Game 2: Head Shoulder Knees Cup		Solo Cups	5 minutes	Selected students
Game 3: Pass the Ball/Tunnel Ball		Gator balls	5 minutes	All students
Game 4: Flag "Football"		Hula Hoops	5 minutes	5 students from each house. Take flag and put in bucket.
Game 5: Hands and Feet Hopscotch		Printouts of Hands & Feet (Adame)	6 minutes	We Are Teachers (40 games to look at later)
9 Week Winner (Prizes) and Presentation of Spirit Winner			5 minutes	

Other Ideas:
- Teacher games and incentives for teachers.
- Creative ways to give points? Action crusader - Have to find.
- Spirit stick winner ideas - Spirit wear, cheering, etc. - add up all points

at the end of the day to announce house winner.
- Next Steps: Students from each grade level house can be recommended by teachers who show that character trait the best from the 9 weeks.

Student Council Ideas:
- They love scarf tag. Lots of kids can play and it is not dangerous.
- Clean Up the Backyard Modified Version: Use a volleyball net and have one house on one side and another house on the other side. It is timed. Kids throw balls to the opposite side. When the timer goes off, the house with the most balls on their side wins.

2nd Rally-December

Setup: 10:00 AM
- AVID Ambassadors, paras, and leadership (specials conference)
- Setup: 4 corners, hang banners, and spirit out (how can we make this better)

Rally Schedule:
- 3-5 Rally: 10:45-11:45
- K-2 Rally: 12:30-1:30

House System Magic: Easy 10-Step Guide to School Spirit

Game/Order	Person Responsible	Items Needed	Time Needed	Notes
Welcome	Welcome Teacher Rep/Oniwon	Music - Bear	10 minutes	
Review of Expectations and Houses				Give house points to groups if following the expectations.
Current Point Standing		Promethean		
Teacher Game		Cup stack		
Game 1: Council Scarf Tag		Hula Hoops	7 minutes	
Game 2: Balloon Hug		Balloons (1 per 2 people)	5 minutes	Look up Kayla Caldwell on TikTok: Christmas Games
Game 3: Clean Up the Backyard Modified Version				Use a volleyball net and have one house on one side and another house on the other side. It is timed. Kids throw balls to the opposite side. When the timer goes off, the house with the most balls on their side wins.
Tallest Tower		Cups with house colors		
Mystery Points				
Draw a Christmas Tree				One partner draws the tree, and partner two draws ornaments. Ornaments have to be on the tree. Count ornaments.
Who Can Spell the Most Christmas Words				
Musical Basketball				Member of each house passes until music stops. Where it stops, that person shoots and gets points for the house.
House Mix and Mingle				Find a member in another house to share a character trait.
Free Play if Time and Weather Permits				
9 Week Winner (Prizes) and Presentation of Spirit Winner			5 minutes	

↓

3rd Rally - March 7th

Rally Schedule:
- K & 1: 11:20-12:20
    - o Opener: Teacher 1
    - o Admin Facilitator: AP
- 2 & 3: 9:00-10:00
    - o Opener: Teacher 2
    - o Admin Facilitator: Principal
- 4 & 5: 10:10-11:10
    - o Opener: Teacher 3
    - o Admin Facilitator: Principal Intern

Specials Lunch: 12:30
Setup: 10:00 AM
- AVID Ambassadors, paras, and leadership (specials conference)
- Setup: 4 corners, hang banners, and spirit out (how can we make this better)

Support:
- Coaches and aides, all available paras, ambassadors, and admin

House System Magic: Easy 10-Step Guide to School Spirit

Game/Order	Person Responsible	Items Needed	Time Needed	Notes
Welcome	Teacher rep/Oniwon	Music - Bear	10 min	
Review of expectations and houses		Promethean		Give house points to groups if they follow expectations. Character trait student example
Teacher game		Hula hoop contest/hippity hop		
Game 1: Wheelbarrow Race		None		Two members race using their bodies as wheelbarrows.
Game 2: Pin the Tail on the Donkey		Poster, blindfolds, cutouts		Stick a cutout of the helmet or shield onto the mascot poster.
Game 3: Simon Says				Whole house or a group of 10 from each house. Last house standing wins.
Musical basketball				Pass until music stops. Where it stops, that person shoots.
Capture the flag		Flags		Protect flag and capture the opposing team's flag without being tagged.
Red light green light				
Rock paper scissors				
House mix and mingle				Find a member in another house to share character trait.
9 week winner (prizes) and presentation of spirit winner			5 min	

Games List and Descriptions
1. Rock Paper Scissors Hula Hoop Jump:
    o   Description: Players jump through hula hoops arranged in a line. At each hoop, they play rock paper scissors with the next person in line. The winner advances, and the loser returns to the start. The game continues until one player reaches the end of the line of hoops.
2. Head Shoulder Knees Cup:
    o   Description: Players stand in front of a cup and follow commands such as "head," "shoulders," and "knees." When "cup" is called, the first player to grab the cup wins. This game tests quick reflexes and listening skills.
3. Pass the Ball/Tunnel Ball:
    o   Description: Teams pass a ball down a line through their legs and over their heads. The first team to get the ball to the end of the line wins. This game encourages teamwork and coordination.
4. Flag "Football":
    o   Description: Players take turns trying to grab a flag from the opponent's bucket and return it to their own without being tagged. This game promotes agility and strategic thinking.
5. Hands and Feet Hopscotch:
    o   Description: Players follow a hopscotch pattern with printouts of hands and feet. They must place their hands and feet on the corresponding printouts as they move through the course. This game enhances coordination and balance.
6. Council Scarf Tag:
    o   Description: Players wear scarves tucked into their waistbands. The objective is to grab as many scarves from other players as possible while protecting your own. The player with the most scarves at the end of the game wins. This game is safe and fun for a large number of participants.
7. Balloon Hug:
    o   Description: Players pair up and place a balloon between their bodies. They must hug the balloon and move together without dropping or popping it. The pair that keeps the balloon intact the longest wins. This game encourages teamwork and physical coordination.
8. Clean Up the Backyard Modified Version:
    o   Description: Use a volleyball net to divide the play area. One house stands on each side. Players throw balls over the net to the opposite side. When the timer goes off, the house with the fewest balls on their side wins. This game emphasizes quick thinking and physical activity.

9. Draw a Christmas Tree:
    o Description: One partner draws the outline of a Christmas tree, and the other partner draws ornaments on it. The challenge is to place the ornaments accurately on the tree. The team with the most well-placed ornaments wins. This game encourages creativity and teamwork.
10. Wheelbarrow Race:
    o Description: Players pair up, with one acting as the "wheelbarrow" and the other as the "driver." The wheelbarrow walks on their hands while the driver holds their legs. The pairs race to the finish line. The first pair to cross the line wins. This game builds strength and coordination.
11. Pin the Tail on the Crusader:
    o Description: Similar to "Pin the Tail on the Donkey," players are blindfolded and must pin a cutout (like a helmet or shield) onto a poster of the Crusader mascot. The player who places the cutout closest to the correct spot wins. This game promotes spatial awareness and fun.
12. Simon Says:
    o Description: The leader gives commands starting with "Simon says." Players must follow the commands only if prefaced by "Simon says." If the leader gives a command without saying "Simon says," players who follow are out. The last player standing wins. This game tests listening skills and concentration.
13. Musical Basketball:
    o Description: Players pass a basketball around while music plays. When the music stops, the player holding the ball must take a shot. If they make the shot, they earn points for their house. This game combines music, movement, and basketball skills.
14. Capture the Flag:
    o Description: Teams are divided, each with a designated flag to protect. Players aim to capture the opposing team's flag and bring it back to their own base without being tagged. This game encourages strategy and teamwork.

These games provide a mix of physical activity, coordination, teamwork, and fun, making them perfect for house rallies and other school events. This is a small sample of some of the games we've played over the years.

House cup and spirit stick.

Blurred to protect student privacy. Check out our Facebook page for images.

Blurred to protect student privacy. Check out our Facebook page for images.

My daughter and I are in the same house.

Greeting students on Wakanda spirit day.

Blurred to protect student privacy. Check out our Facebook page for images.

Purchased from Amazon

Blurred to protect student privacy. Check out our Facebook page for images.

Rallies Unifying Moments: Planning Exciting House Rallies

Questions for Reflection:

1. How often will you hold house rallies, and what is the best timing for your school?

2. How can you group students to ensure fair and fun competition?

3. What methods can you use to involve the entire campus community in planning and executing rallies?

4. How will you decorate and set up the rally space to maximize excitement?

5. Who will host and facilitate the rallies, and how will you support them?

6. What types of games will you include, and how will you ensure they are suitable for all age groups?

7. How will you manage transitions between activities to keep the energy high?

8. What incentives and rewards will you provide to maintain student engagement and enthusiasm?

Reflect on these questions to tailor your house rallies to your school's unique needs and resources, ensuring they are both fun and effective.

8 STUDENT INVOLVEMENT FOSTERING ENGAGEMENT: MAXIMIZING STUDENT PARTICIPATION

Involving students in your house system is crucial for its success. Throughout previous chapters, we've discussed various ways to integrate student participation, but let's bring it all together here.

Importance of Student Involvement
Student involvement is the heartbeat of a thriving house system. When students are actively engaged, they take ownership of the program, which boosts their enthusiasm and commitment. Involving students fosters a sense of community, encourages leadership, and enhances the overall school culture.

How We Involve Students
1. Leadership Roles:
   o We use students who are already members of our campus leadership teams, such as the student council, AVID ambassadors, and the tech team. These students assist with rally planning and implementation.
2. House Selection:
   o During the selection rally, students go down a giant slide and select their house card from a cup at the end. This exciting process sets the tone for their involvement in the house system.
3. Rally Participation:
   o Students participate in various games and activities during rallies. Each game involves multiple students from each house, ensuring broad participation.
   o Cheerleaders and student leaders help with setting up and transitioning between games.
4. Character Trait Examples:
   o At the beginning of each rally, a student from each house shares an example of how they exhibited their house's character trait during the nine weeks.
5. Spirit Week:
   o Leading up to the house selection day, each day of the week is assigned to a house. Teachers and students in that house dress up and decorate the campus in their house colors. This creates

excitement and anticipation for the selection rally.

Additional Ideas for Student Involvement
1. House Committees:
   o Form house committees where students can take on specific roles, such as planning events, managing house communication, and coordinating spirit activities.
2. Mentorship Programs:
   o Pair older students with younger ones in a mentorship program within the house system. This fosters relationships and provides guidance and support for younger students.
3. Student-Led Assemblies:
   o Allow students to lead assemblies and rallies, giving them the opportunity to develop public speaking and organizational skills.
4. House Challenges:
   o Organize monthly house challenges that involve academic, artistic, and athletic activities. This can include everything from spelling bees to art contests to sports tournaments.
5. Feedback Sessions:
   o Hold regular feedback sessions with students to gather their input on the house system. This helps ensure the program remains relevant and engaging.

House System Magic: Easy 10-Step Guide to School Spirit

Student Involvement Fostering Engagement: Maximizing Student Participation

Questions for Reflection:

1. How can you create leadership opportunities for students within your house system?

2. What methods can you use to ensure broad and diverse student participation in house activities?

3. How can you integrate house-related activities into your existing school schedule?

4. What new ideas can you implement to increase student involvement in your house system?

5. How will you measure the impact of student involvement on the success of the house system?

Reflecting on these questions will help you tailor your house system to fit the unique needs and dynamics of your school, ensuring maximum student engagement and success.

9 ENVIRONMENT CREATING A VIBRANT ATMOSPHERE: SETTING THE STAGE FOR SUCCESS

Creating an engaging and visually stimulating environment is key to the success of your house system. The way you display house-related materials can significantly impact student enthusiasm and school spirit. Here's how we've done it, and a few ideas to inspire you to create a vibrant house system environment.

Our House System Environment
In our hall, we have a huge bulletin board that features each house's banner along with photos from house rallies. This bulletin board also serves as the display for the house points. Our office aide updates the point totals daily, ensuring that the competition stays lively and current. We're still brainstorming ways to make this point display more interactive and fun for the students.
In front of the bulletin board, there's a table that proudly houses the House Cup. The House Cup sits in front of the banner of the house that won the previous nine weeks, staying there for a full nine weeks until the next winner is announced. This prominent display is a constant reminder of the friendly competition and motivates students to strive for excellence.

We've seen campuses that have entire hallways dedicated to their house systems, with extensive decorations and themed areas. While that's fantastic, remember to do what works for you and your school. The key is to create an environment that your students will find inspiring and that fits within your resources.

On our PBIS posters, we have four Crusaders (our mascot) at the bottom of each poster, each holding a shield representing one of the houses. This small touch helps to integrate the house system into our broader PBIS framework.
Outside of these elements, we don't have much campus decor specifically dedicated to the house system. We believe in starting small and building up as we see what resonates best with our students and staff.

Ideas for Enhancing Your House System Environment
1. House Hallways:
    o Dedicate a hallway or section of your school to each house. Decorate with house colors, banners, and student artwork. This can create a sense of pride and ownership among

students.
2. Interactive Displays:
   o Incorporate interactive elements into your bulletin boards, such as wheels of fortune for house points, or digital displays that show live updates of house standings.
3. Themed Classrooms:
   o Encourage teachers to adopt a house theme in their classrooms. This can include color-coordinated decorations, posters, and classroom supplies.
4. House Murals:
   o Commission student artists to create murals for each house. These can depict the house mascot, values, and notable achievements.
5. House Spirit Days:
   o Designate specific days for students and staff to wear their house colors and decorate their classrooms or workspaces accordingly.

Environment Creating a Vibrant Atmosphere: Setting the Stage for Success

Questions for Reflection:

1. How can you creatively display house points to maintain student interest and engagement?

2. What areas of your school could be dedicated to house-specific decorations and displays?

3. How can you involve students in creating and maintaining house-related decorations?

4. What small changes can you implement to integrate the house system into your existing school environment?

5. How will you measure the impact of these environmental changes on school spirit and student engagement?

By reflecting on these questions and experimenting with different ideas, you can create a vibrant and dynamic environment that truly brings your house system to life. Remember, the goal is to make the house system a visible and exciting part of your school culture, so don't be afraid to get creative and have fun with it!

10 MISCELLANEOUS TIPS EXTRA INSIGHTS: HANDY TIPS FOR A SMOOTH IMPLEMENTATION

Welcome to the final chapter! We're wrapping up with some handy tips and extra insights to ensure your house system runs smoothly and remains engaging for everyone involved. Let's make this fun and memorable!

Handy Tips for a Smooth Implementation

- Chants and Mottos:
    - Each house has a motto. You can find them on our house cards in chapter three. Use these mottos to create house chants and build team spirit.
- Video Announcements:
    - We record video announcements once a week. Each day, we remind students of a house character trait and inform them of house totals. This keeps everyone in the loop and motivated.
- Backpack Tags:
    - Students have a backpack tag that identifies their house. This is especially useful for dismissal when giving out points. We bought these tags in bulk from Amazon; they are simply the house cards on a tag.
- Use Social Media:
    - I'm including a QR code to our Facebook page so you can check out pictures of our rallies and some decor. Please note, we don't include student faces in this book for privacy reasons.
- House Shirts:
    - Shirts are not required. As a Title I school, we understand that not all parents can afford them. We partnered with a local shirt printing company that designed the shirts and sells them for us. Parents can choose pick-up or shipping, and we are not involved in this process at all. Of course, you could do shirt orders, sell them, or have your PTO handle it, but we try to keep our process as simple as possible.
    - Parents sometimes make their own shirts, and we encourage students who don't have shirts to wear their house colors on spirit days. Students also wear their house shirts on Fridays, fostering a sense of unity and pride.

- o Here are the key points to remember:
- o House shirts are optional, and students can wear their house colors instead.
- o A local printing company designs and sells the shirts, with pick-up or shipping options.
- o The school is not involved in the sales process to keep it simple.
- o Students proudly wear their house shirts on Fridays to show their house spirit.
- Incorporate AI:
  - o When deciding on names, mottos, changes, character traits, and other things, use AI and ChatGPT. I recommend this for many things outside of the house system. Our jobs are hard—save some time!
  - o Prompts for AI:
    - ▪ "Generate creative house names and mottos for a school house system."
    - ▪ "What are some engaging house rally game ideas for elementary students?"
    - ▪ "How can we visually display house points in a fun and interactive way?"
- Have Fun and Remember Your Purpose:
  - o Always keep the fun in the house system. Remember why you're doing this—to build community, foster character, and enhance school spirit. Don't stress about competing with other campuses. Each system is unique, and so is every campus.
- Flexibility is Key:
  - o Be open to learning and adapting. We are four years in and are still learning. Your system will evolve as you see what works best for your community.

Closing Thoughts

As we conclude, keep in mind that this is just one way—our way. This is our simplified version that works best for our budget, personnel, and campus improvement goals. It's not meant to be a comprehensive guide, but rather a source of inspiration. You can scale this back or take ideas and make them as extra as you like. We are not the house gurus! There are campuses doing way more than we are. But if you're like me, and you want a house system that may be a little more manageable, these steps may work for you. I hope you feel equipped and inspired to implement a house system that brings your school community closer together. The key is to make it fun, meaningful, and tailored to your unique campus. Here's to creating lasting memories and fostering a supportive, spirited school environment!

Extra Tips Recap:
- Use house mottos and chants to build team spirit.
- Record weekly video announcements for updates.
- Implement backpack tags for easy house identification.
- Share your journey on social media, but respect privacy.
- Leverage AI for brainstorming and efficiency.
- Keep it fun, remember your purpose, and don't compete with others.
- Stay flexible and open to learning.

Example Prompts for AI:
1. "Generate creative house names and mottos for a school house system."
2. "What are some engaging house rally game ideas for elementary students?"
3. "How can we visually display house points in a fun and interactive way?"

Remember, every system is unique, and so is every campus. Enjoy the journey and make it your own!

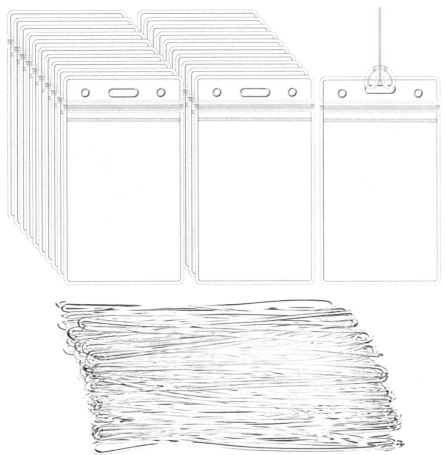

These are the tags we use for backpacks, made from the house cards that students pull from the cup. We purchase these tags in bulk from Amazon.

Crockett Elementary
Published by Tailis Oniwon
· October 12, 2023 ·

Friday is rally day!
Please wear your house shirt or colors. We are looking for EXTRA spirit (face paint, tutus, pompoms, etc.) Any one with extra spirit will earn additional points for his/her house. Let's see who takes the cup this nine weeks! 🖤🖤🖤🖤

This is an example of a social media post from the day before a rally.

Crockett Elementary
Published by Tailis Oniwon

September 1, 2023 ·

Our first house rally is 9/15. Use the links below to order house shirts.
All kinder and new students will go down the slide on 9/15 to select their houses. We ask that students not in a house wear a white shirt that can be marked on 😜

Here are the 4 links to our website or they can search the house name and it will show up 😜

WAKANDA- https://countrygonecrazy.com/.../wakanda-t-shirt-crockett...

Wakanda T-Shirt - Crockett Elementary
This t-shirt is made with a DTF (direct to film) transfer. 🤍 The design is pressed onto a Black Gildan SoftStyle T-Shirt - 100% Cotton - fits true to size 🤍
countrygonecrazy.com

ARAGON-https://countrygonecrazy.com/.../aragon-t-shirt-crockett...

Aragon T-Shirt - Crockett Elementary
This t-shirt is made with a DTF (direct to film) transfer. 🤍 The design is pressed onto a Black Gildan SoftStyle T-Shirt - 100% Cotton - fits true to size 🤍
countrygonecrazy.com

IGNITE-https://countrygonecrazy.com/.../ignite-t-shirt-crockett...

Ignite T-Shirt - Crockett Elementary
This t-shirt is made with a DTF (direct to film) transfer. 🤍 The design is pressed onto a Black Gildan SoftStyle T-Shirt - 100% Cotton - fits true to size 🤍
countrygonecrazy.com

LIGHTNING-https://countrygonecrazy.com/.../lightning-t-shirt...

Lightning T-Shirt - Crockett Elementary
This t-shirt is made with a DTF (direct to film) transfer. 🤍 The design is pressed onto a Black Gildan SoftStyle T-Shirt - 100% Cotton - fits true to size 🤍
countrygonecrazy.com

This is how we sell our shirts without involving the campus or PTO in the process.

Scan the QR code to check out our Facebook page for more photos of our rallies and other PBIS adventures.

House System Magic: A Planning Checklist

Step 1: Introduction

Welcome to House System Magic: A 10-Step Guide to School Spirit

- o   Read the introduction and familiarize yourself with the guide's purpose.

- o   Set a goal for transforming your school's culture.

"Education is the most powerful weapon which you can use to change the world." - Nelson Mandela

Notes:

_____

_____

_____

House System Magic: Easy 10-Step Guide to School Spirit

Step 2: Setting the Foundation

Understand the Benefits

- o Review the core benefits with your team.

    - o Boosts school spirit and student engagement

    - o Encourages positive behavior and academic achievement

    - o Fosters a sense of community and belonging

- o Discuss how these benefits align with your school's goals.

"The whole purpose of education is to turn mirrors into windows." - Sydney J. Harris

Notes:

_____

_____

_____

Step 3: Crafting House Identities

Create Memorable House Names and Emblems

- o   Brainstorm house themes with staff and students.

- o   Choose themes relevant to your school's culture.

- o   Design house emblems and colors.

"A person's name is to him or her the sweetest and most important sound in any language."
- Dale Carnegie

Notes:

_____

_____

_____

Step 4: Leadership and Assignments

Select and Empower House Leaders

o   Identify dynamic leaders among students and staff.

o   Provide training and support to house leaders.

Fair House Assignments

o   Ensure balanced distribution of students across houses.

"A leader is one who knows the way, goes the way, and shows the way." - John C. Maxwell

Notes:

_____

_____

_____

Step 5: Tracking and Rewards

Implement a Point System

- o   Use tools like Class Dojo to track house points.

- o   Define clear criteria for earning points.

Plan Exciting House Rallies

- o   Organize events that encourage participation and boost morale.

"Success is the sum of small efforts, repeated day in and day out." - Robert Collier

Notes:

_____

_____

_____

Step 6: Encouraging Participation

Ensure Active Student Participation

o Involve students in decision-making processes.

o Create opportunities for student ownership and responsibility.

Celebrate Achievements

o Display house achievements prominently around the school.

"Tell me and I forget, teach me and I remember, involve me and I learn." - Benjamin Franklin

Notes:

_____

_____

_____

Step 7: Review and Adjust

Review and Adjust Regularly

- o   Gather feedback from students and staff.

- o   Make necessary adjustments to improve the system.

Maintain Momentum

- o   Schedule regular review meetings.

- o   Plan a yearly calendar of house events.

"The secret of getting ahead is getting started." - Mark Twain

Notes:

_____

_____

_____

Conclusion

Congratulations! You are now equipped with a comprehensive plan to implement a vibrant house system in your school. Remember, the key to success is continuous engagement and celebration of achievements. Good luck on your journey to building school spirit!

Contact Information: For further assistance, please reach out to: Tailis Oniwon

Email: tailisoniwon@yahoo.com

Feel free to adjust any sections as needed to better suit your specific needs and school environment!

ABOUT THE AUTHOR

Tailis Oniwon is a dedicated wife and mother of four beautiful children. With a career spanning 14 years in education, Tailis has spent 7 of those years as an administrator, where her passion for fostering a positive school culture

has shone brightly. Throughout her illustrious career, she has been recognized with numerous accolades, including District Teacher of the Year, District Principal of the Year, District ESL Teacher of the Year, and as a HAABSE finalist.

A proud graduate of Texas Southern University, Tailis holds a bachelor's degree in early childhood education and a master's degree in administration. Her commitment to education is evident in her tireless efforts to create engaging, inclusive, and dynamic learning environments for her students and staff.

Tailis's love for education is matched by her enthusiasm for reading, watching shows, and traveling during her leisure time. She continues to inspire and lead, making education not just a profession but a lifelong passion.